IRONMASTER

The Life and Times of John Wilkinson

By
Richard Unwin

All rights reserved. No part of this publication may be reproduced, stored in a retrieval system or transmitted in any form, or by any means, electronic mechanical, photocopying, recording, or otherwise, without the prior permission of the copyright holder.

Web Site - www.quoadultra.net

Copyright © Richard Unwin 2010

CONTENTS

IRONMASTER 1
INTRODUCTION 4
ISAAC WILKINSON 7
MAKING IRON 12
THE EIGHTEENTH CENTURY IRON INDUSTRY . 17
THE IRONMASTER...19
DISSENTERS IN THE EIGHTEENTH CENTURY ...21
ENGINES OF MORTALITY 26
BORING STEAM ENGINE CYLINDERS.................30
JOHN WILKINSON'S STEAM ENGINES 36
THE TRIAL...41
THE IRON BUSINESS 45
IRON MAD 53
BIBLIOGRAPHY 57
   Books By the Same Author 59

INTRODUCTION

Gold and silver have been worshipped for their ornament and for the wealth attached to them, copper and tin for their utilitarianism, but iron is part of the soul; it is elemental, of the earth and as common as the clay from which mankind was formed. All other metals are subject to iron. Gold and silver are easier to wrest from the earth with iron tools; the sword has won the wealth of nations, the earth encouraged to fertility by the iron plough and harvested with the sickle.

The oldest crafts are those of the iron-founder and the smith. In antiquity, the Smith was deemed to have magical powers. He could take this plain metal, extracted from the stones of the earth, and forge it using air and fire before quenching it in water, these being regarded as magical elements, to produce tools, weapons and ornaments that were worn by the highest in the tribe. In legend, Wayland the Smith is enshrined on a par with Arthur's Merlin. On the Ridgeway (now in Oxfordshire, once in Berkshire), near the White Horse, Wayland is still reputed to have his smithy although now hidden from mortal eyes. This worker in iron was so important, that his king had him crippled to make it impossible for him to run away. It is said that if a horse loses a shoe, a traveller may leave his horse tethered by Wayland's Smithy overnight, with a silver coin beneath the cast shoe, and in the morning the horse will be shod. Such is the aura of mystique that surrounds the craft of iron making. It was not until mankind discovered how to smelt and forge this common yet extraordinary metal that progress towards the modern world could begin. The craft was so important that the period which first discovered how to extract and use it was named The Iron Age.

At first, iron could only be smelted in small quantities and the cost of its production was enormous. Early furnaces for extracting iron were fuelled by charcoal and it took six tons of charcoal to produce one ton of iron. Wood was a universal building material used for housing, transport, machinery and fuel. The extra demands made by the charcoal burner soon denuded the forests and woodlands of Europe. When, in 1709 Abraham Darby discovered how to smelt iron using coal instead of wood, the way was open for the creation of a new age of iron. Within a few years iron was being produced in hitherto unimagined quantities and a new industry was being forged, that of - The Ironmaster! John Wilkinson was an enigmatic character. Although he is frequently mentioned in association with the famous names of his time - James Watt, Abraham Darby, John Smeaton, Thomas Telford etc., his contribution to engineering history has never had the popular prominence given to others. Perhaps this is because he did not introduce fundamentally new inventions and many of his ideas were improvements on the work of his father, Isaac Wilkinson. John was more of an innovator. Technically brilliant, he used and improved the new devices and inventions of his day in a way that pioneered their use. Without people like John Wilkinson, these new devices would have been only slowly introduced, if at all. John's father, Isaac, was not a particularly good businessman; it was John who was the entrepreneur of the family. Had it not been for the commercial skills of industrialist Matthew Boulton, and John Wilkinson's technical brilliance, Watt's greatly improved steam engine would not have enjoyed commercial success and the symbol for work energy would not today be the Watt. This is not to say that John did not produce any firsts. He was the first to launch an iron boat, "The Trial" on the River Severn and his name appears with that of Abraham Darby III in the list of subscribers to the building project that was to construct the world's first iron bridge. He improved the boring bar which he used to bore cannon and was the first to adapt it to produce a precision bore in a steam engine cylinder.

This aspect of Wilkinson's character is important, as early industry could not have developed without those who were willing to embrace new ideas and find practical means to apply them. Others were looking to make their fortunes by exploiting the new inventions that were coming on to the industrial scene. Watt had demonstrated that, as the patent holder for the operating principle of his steam engine, no one else could use the invention without paying him a royalty. Of course, Watt had patented his ideas. Others were not so scrupulous. If someone could get hold of an idea and apply for a patent before the actual inventor, then, should the invention prove to be a commercial success, they could net a fortune. Some were not too particular as to how they obtained a new patent and pirating the ideas of others made several fortunes. Where a patented device was successful the unscrupulous would try to get around the patent, not always legitimately, or simply build a machine without paying the necessary royalties. This was an era when industrial espionage was practised blatantly and would continue vigorously through the Georgian and Victorian periods to the present day.

The lack of general engineering knowledge among the populace allowed dishonest entrepreneurs to extract money from gullible investors on the basis of a spurious but plausible description of a machine or process. The commercial success enjoyed by Watt dazzled the innocent and spurred on the greedy. Manufacturing industry in the eighteenth century was a combination of practicality and mystique. Machinery was becoming more complex, but relied on water and animal power for motivation. John Wilkinson developed the expertise to bore accurately Watt's steam engine cylinders; he also cast valve chests and other components essential to the operation of these machines. Wilkinson was quick to take up the ideas of Watt and he was the first ironmaster to order and build a Watt engine to provide the forced draught in his ironworks at Broseley in Shropshire. John ordered further engines from Boulton and Watt, indicating that he could see their potential and knew how to get the best out of them.

As well as being a supplier of guns to the Royal Navy, John Wilkinson traded with several other countries, which, coupled with his views on religion and the Crown, led to suspicions about his loyalty. He was a religious Dissenter in an age that was less than tolerant of religions other than that of the Church of England. In 1745, there had been a rebellion by the Jacobites that had unnerved the establishment and thrown suspicion on all Dissenters. The fact that John Wilkinson, helped by his brother William, developed a thriving business with iron foundries in England and in France shows what a remarkable personality he must have had. Known as Iron Mad Wilkinson, he had several iron coffins made for his own eventual use - one at each of his houses. He would proudly show these off to his guests and offer to make one for them. He pioneered the use of iron in all areas - decorative, constructional and mechanical. He suggested the use of iron in house building and even made an iron pulpit.

When he died a very wealthy man in 1808, he was buried in his iron coffin in the grounds of his house at Castlehead near Grange-over-Sands. Over his grave was erected an iron obelisk inscribed with an epitaph he had written himself. The obelisk survives and has been restored to stand just outside the village of Lindale on the road to Grange-over-Sands. Today, John Wilkinson lies in an unmarked grave in Lindale churchyard.

ISAAC WILKINSON

In the year 1728, the wagon trails leading over the Cumbrian fells in the north-western fringes of the English Lake District were only a little less rough than the country they crossed. On one particular day in this year a heavily pregnant woman was jolted and shaken along such a trail as she rode a wagon home from the market at Workington. The jolting must have induced labour for the wagon had to stop while she gave birth, beside the trail, to a healthy baby boy. The woman was the wife of Isaac Wilkinson and the baby boy was later christened John. The Wilkinson's lived in the village of Little Clifton, just a few miles from Workington. Reputedly, the women of the village prophesied over the baby boy that "t'lad wod sum day be a gurt man." If this is to be believed then the village women were indeed prophets because the boy did become a "gurt" (great) man - in fact, he grew up to be one of the greatest ironmasters of his time. During the eighty years of his life the iron industry would grow in much the same way as the computer industry has developed in the second half of the twentieth century. Early in the eighteenth century iron production for the whole of England was less than 17,000 tons whereas in 1808, the year of John Wilkinson's death, the figure had risen to 250,000 tons. Isaac's first son was to play a major part in producing this increase.

It is not known where Isaac Wilkinson originated. In 1728, the year of his first son's birth, Isaac was registered as a foundry workman at Little Clifton and he was earning a guinea a week. A guinea was a lot of money in those days and so he would have either been employed in a responsible position, or he had special skills or knowledge to sell. In addition to his foundry work, he also occupied a small farm. The village was the location of a charcoal-fuelled blast furnace and this must have been why Isaac had chosen to live there. When John was about twelve years old the family moved to Backbarrow in the Furness District of Cumberland. There was an iron furnace, opposite which Isaac took a house, "Bare Syke." Known at this time as "a pot-founder" Isaac, assisted by John, would bring the molten iron from the furnace in a ladle and pour it into moulds in the workshop attached to the house. Obviously, by this time Isaac had decided to work independently. Records show that he purchased the molten iron from the foundry and sold back the finished product. Isaac Wilkinson's speciality was the making of smoothing irons. At Backbarrow, his products were ordinary smoothing irons but later he invented a method that allowed hollow box irons to be cast in one piece, which made them easier to, manufacture. The business must have been profitable as it paid for the education of his sons.

Isaac had three sons and two daughters. John was the eldest with William being born later to a second wife. A third son, Henry, died a young man. Of his two daughters, Mary married the distinguished Dr. Joseph Priestly, a Unitarian Minister and scientist, while another daughter married a man named Jones. After John's death, in 1808, this nephew (having changed his name to Wilkinson) engaged in destructive litigation over John Wilkinson's estate. The Wilkinson's were dissenters - that is, people whose religious views did not conform to those of the Church of England. It is not clear exactly which faith Isaac followed, but the family certainly had close connections with a variety of dissenters. Dissenting groups were Catholics, Unitarians, Presbyterians, Quakers and, later in the century, the Methodists.

Because of their isolation from the mainstream of English society, dissenters tended to live together in close communities and formed family ties and business links with each other. They generally believed in personal honesty and hard work, qualities which, along with a commercially biased education, tended to make of them successful business people. It was to one of the dissenting academies, that of Dr. Caleb Rotherham at Kendal, that John was sent to receive his education. John's brother, William, when he reached school age, went to Dr. Joseph Priestly a Unitarian Minister who had a school at Nantwich, in Cheshire, and later an academy at Warrington.

When John left Dr. Rotherham's academy, he was apprenticed to an ironmonger in Liverpool and it is probably here that he honed his considerable business skills. Five years later he returned home to find his father had acquired his own furnace at Wilson House on the River Winster near Cartmel. At this time charcoal was still being used as a fuel for iron making. Practically every industry needed wood - carpentry, building, shipbuilding, wagon making and so on, providing competition which made charcoal expensive and hard to obtain. Interruptions in supplies of charcoal would be frequent making planned production difficult. Another problem was that once a furnace had been put into blast it had to be kept charged with ore and fuel as the job of getting it up to temperature was time consuming and expensive. Isaac clearly had a pioneering spirit and the reason that he had erected a furnace at Wilson House was that the surrounding area was a peat bog. He had the idea that if peat could be used as a fuel, he would reduce his operating costs and make the supply of fuel more certain. The peat was cut from the surrounding bog and cut into bricks, which were then dried in the sun, compressed and charred. The experiment, however, was not a success and from this time began the slow decline of Isaac's fortunes. The peat was cut from channels that quickly flooded. An ingenious use was made of this in that barges were floated in the channels to transport peat from the diggings. There is a local story that Isaac built an iron barge for use in the channels and that it remains there to this day, sunken beneath the peat beside the River Winster. Although it is unlikely that an actual iron barge was constructed, it is possible that some of the components of a barge were made of iron and perhaps, in remembering his father's experiments, this inspired John to build the first iron boat "The Trial" and successfully launch it on the River Severn many years later.

In his early twenties John went into Staffordshire which was the centre of the iron smelting trade. Here he would have been introduced to the principle of smelting iron using coke rather than charcoal as a fuel. Earlier experiments by ironfounders using coal had failed, but around 1709, Abraham Derby 1st obtained coke by roasting the coal to remove its impurities. The coke fuel produced iron of marketable quality and the process was to ultimately break the tyranny of charcoal allowing cheaper iron to be smelted in larger quantities. Back at Wilson House Isaac was still busily putting his inventive mind to the introduction of new products. In 1753 he took out a patent for "a new sort of cast metallick roll for crushing, flattening, bruising, or grinding of malt, hops beans or any kind of grain, and also for crushing, bruising, or grinding of sugar canes."

It was in this year that Isaac first became connected with the iron works at Bersham, near Wrexham, where he introduced yet another innovation. Blast furnaces use air from large bellows through an aperture called a tuyere (pronounced tweer). Cams that were driven by a water wheel operated the bellows. This was often inconvenient as the water wheel had to be located near to the furnaces, which was not always feasible. At Bersham, in 1757, Isaac developed and patented the use of a remote draught system where the air blast was delivered to the furnaces through a pipeline, using the weight of water alone as the means of providing draught. This meant the furnaces and the water wheel could be more conveniently placed to suit their different modes of operation. The excavated remains of the old iron works at Bersham can be seen today and there is a short section, possibly of Isaac's blast pipe, remaining. From the details in his patent, it seems that the "bellows" were some kind of displacement pump as the air is described as being forced through the pipeline by the pressure of water. An arrangement of siphons, cocks and valves was used to get the water in cisterns to alternately rise and fall displacing the air to produce a continuous draught. Isaac Wilkinson took out his last patent in 1758. It was for: *"A new method or invention for casting of guns or cannon, fire engine cylinders, pipes and sugar rolls and other such like instruments, in dried sand, in iron boxes made for that purpose, whereby the said guns, &c., will be made and cast in a much more neat, compleat, exact and useful, as well as cheap and expeditious manner, than any method hitherto known and made use of."*

The patent went on to describe the method: *"The outside or cope of the mould or moulds in which the guns or cannon, fire engine cylinders, pipes and sugar rolls, or such like instruments, or any of them, is or are intended to be cast must be made of sand mixt with a little horse or cow dung, or any other thing to make it porous. This sand is made wett and then rammed up, the patern being first put in iron boxes made for that purpose, of 2,3,4,5 or any no. of parts or pieces as the nature of the instrument to be cast requires: then the boxes are to be taken asunder into pieces and the patern taken out; then the sand in the boxes is dried in a stove and when dry it must be blackened or faced with some wett charcoal dust, or black lead or any other mixture or thing to make the sand come of or part from the metal when cast. The insides or cords of all the different instruments above mentioned are made with iron bars, either hollow and full of holes, or sollid and traced or fluted, and if the bore is large it may be made of bricks walled, and the barrs of iron or bricks are to be wraped round with ropes made of straw or hay, to take the air of, and must then be covered with a proper thickness of the said sand, and then dried and blacked, as before directed; and then the moulds are put together and the instruments cast, and bored, and turned as required."*

This patent mentions the casting of cannon, an operation that was to become one of the Wilkinsons' most profitable products. Although Isaac was extremely inventive and ingenious, about 1761 the business at Bersham ran into difficulty and by 1762 Isaac had to bring the operation to a close. The exact circumstances are not known, but Isaac left Bersham and is thought to have gone to Bristol. What is known is that his sons William, and John, who had been helping him since 1756, took over the business and from that point onwards it began to thrive! It seems that Bersham was manufacturing box-heaters, calendar rolls, malt-mill rolls, sugar rolls, pipes, shells, grenades and guns.

All of these products had come from the inventive brain of Isaac. John, however, was able to make further improvements to these that were to ensure his success as an ironmaster.

MAKING IRON

By the Middle-Ages iron had become a common essential metal; it was used in agriculture, for building and for weapons and armour. Horses needed shoes to carry knights into battle and to enable them to work pulling the plough. The main iron producing areas in England during the Middle-Ages were in the Forest of Dean and the Weald in Sussex. It was from the sixty or so forges in the Forest of Dean that Richard 1 once ordered the mass production of fifty thousand horse-shoes. Most imported iron came from Spain with smaller amounts coming from Sweden and Normandy. Imported iron was, of course, much more expensive than that produced in England, and English iron was roughly ten times more expensive than that produced today. Tools were usually made of wood and tipped with iron only at their wear sides or their cutting edges.

Knowledge of iron working reached Britain about 400 BC. The iron ore was mixed with charcoal and heated in a fire-bowl where the heat was intensified using hand-operated bellows. This method could not generate sufficient heat to liquefy the iron but a spongy mass known as bloom was produced. The bloom was beaten until the cinder and other impurities were driven out. The resulting wrought iron was then reheated and beaten into shape in a blacksmith's forge. The early swords were made of bronze with steel only on the cutting edges. The early English poem Beowulf describes such a sword: "Beowulf's sword, iron-edged, had injured the guardian of the hoard . . ."

Water power began to be used in the Middle-Ages to operate trip hammers for working the bloom and crushing the crude ore. Trip hammers could be made heavier than those wielded by the smith in his forge and they provided more blows per minute. This represented a great step forward in the manufacture of iron. The first furnace to use water power for operating bellows to increase the draught was built in 1323, raising the temperature to 1500oC. For the first time, iron could be melted and poured as a liquid into moulds. In 1380 the first real blast furnace was built.

The area of Westmoreland where the Wilkinson's were first recorded as living has long associations with the making of iron. Furness Abbey, founded in 1127, is located on a peninsula that extends into the northern part of Morecambe Bay. The peninsular is so pronounced that in the Middle-Ages the abbey is recorded, in a petition by the abbot to Henry IV, as being on an island - "*assis en une isle.*" The main road to Furness in the Middle-Ages was across the deadly Morecambe Sands - at low tide of course. One way in which the Normans controlled the region was by the establishment of monastic houses. There were twelve monastic houses in all. Furness Abbey, with its principal estates in High and Low Furness, was the second wealthiest in England after Fountains Abbey. It was run by the Cistercians who had a long and proficient knowledge of iron making. Many Cistercian houses would have had a bloomery and forge attached, operated by water-powered trip hammers, where they would make iron for their own use exporting any surplus. The monasteries were large scale trading and farming units - the industrial estates of their day. Though the mainstay of their wealth was in wool production, the reason that Furness Abbey was the second wealthiest in England was because, in addition to traditional products, it profited from iron making. Iron ore was extracted from around Dalton and taken to High Furness where there was plenty of charcoal.

The making of iron is a multi-stage process. The method used from the beginning of the sixteenth century was to first smelt ore in a blast furnace using charcoal as a fuel. The liquid iron was cast into depressions made in sand and became known as pig iron. The term pig iron arises from the shape of the moulds, which were arranged either side of a centre channel into which the molten iron was poured from the furnace. The arrangement of the moulds was similar to the sight of piglets feeding from a sow and so the name stuck. Although iron could be poured directly into moulds as cast iron, in order to obtain the quality required for tool-making and other uses the iron had to go through further processes. Pig iron was taken from the furnaces and distributed to forges where it was re-worked and made into the end product - wrought iron. Large-scale production of wrought iron only began in the closing years of the eighteenth century and the beginning of the nineteenth century, but these early developments paved the way for later mass production. At the forge the pig iron was heated in a finery hearth fired with charcoal where the temperature was raised using an air blast from bellows. The finer, the person who worked the hearth, would stir the molten metal with an iron bar so that oxygen in the air would combine with carbon in the iron to produce a crude type of wrought iron. Iron was drawn off the finery hearth and allowed to cool into a soft mass. In this state it would be hammered into a rectangular shape known as a bloom.

Mechanical power to generate the air blast for the finery hearth and the hammer of the forge would be provided by a water wheel. A bloom of iron was not much use to the iron-working craftsmen and so it was necessary to process it further. A chafery furnace, which was similar to a finery but without the air blast, would heat the iron bloom to a workable condition. When it was hot enough it would be hammered to a shape that could be passed between rollers to produce a thin sheet. It was then taken to the slitting mill where it was passed between rotating discs that cut it into bars suitable for use by smiths and other iron-working craftsmen. Rollers could shape hot iron where the formed profile of the bar would give it some required additional strength.

A Slitting and Rolling Mill

Iron is extracted from its ore in the blast furnace. This is a tall furnace, lined with firebrick and charged with the ore, fuel and limestone. At first only charcoal could be used as a fuel because other fuels, such as coal, contained impurities that would contaminate the iron. Limestone was used as a flux to separate the molten iron from the ore. There were three holes at the base of a blast furnace - one for tapping the iron, another for tapping off the slag and a third (the tuyere) for the air blast. Tap holes were blocked by clay plugs until needed. First the furnace would be charged with the iron ore, charcoal and limestone. Once fired, the furnace would operate continuously. An air blast would be introduced to the furnace through the tuyere. As the temperature increased the iron and limestone would melt. As iron is heavy, it would form into a separate liquid pool in the bottom of the furnace while floating above were the impurities from the ore and fuel, contained in the lighter slag formed by the molten limestone. When sufficient iron had been produced it would be tapped off into the casting bed. Slag was tapped off and discarded. The furnace was then charged with more fuel, ore and limestone and the process repeated.

Charcoal was used for fuel, not only because of its purity, but because it burns at a temperature of 1100 degrees Celsius. Ten tons of wood was needed to produce two-and-a-half tons of charcoal. It took six tons of charcoal to produce one ton of iron. Charcoal is made by a very old and skilled process. First the charcoal burner would mark out a circular area with a diameter of up to sixteen feet (4.8 metres). Next he would dig a shallow pit and build over it a thick cone of cord wood. (Cord wood is tree trunks of medium diameter that are sawn into uniform lengths). The centre of the stack would be formed to provide a chimney then closed by inserting a "motty peg". Finally, he would cover the stacked woodpile with turf and soil but leave ventilation holes at intervals around the circumference. The stack was fired by dropping burning embers of charcoal down the hole exposed by removing the "motty peg". When the stack was alight the chimney hole was covered with an iron lid. Smoke would issue from the ventilation holes, the colour of which indicated when the charcoal was ready. This would take three or four days and the charcoal burner had to constantly tend the stack, and others he might be working on, to ensure a slow combustion of the wood. When the colour of the smoke turned from white to blue, the charcoal burner blocked off all the ventilation holes and let the stack cool for several days before breaking it open to extract the charcoal.

Wood was used for many other purposes and charcoal, as a fuel, became very expensive and hard to obtain. When, in 1709, Abraham Darby successfully smelted iron using coke as a fuel, the way was open for the expansion of a dynamic and important industry. The furnace it is thought he used is at Coalbrookdale, near Ironbridge, in Shropshire.

The site has been excavated and protected by a special building. Coalbrookdale had been an important iron and steel producing area from the early sixteenth century and was to become, in the century after Abraham Darby's new process was introduced, one of the most important industrial sites in the world.

THE EIGHTEENTH CENTURY IRON INDUSTRY

At the beginning of the 18th century the iron industry was heavily reliant on the supply of charcoal and the availability of water power. The problems of charcoal supply have already been described and were only partly solved when coke was introduced as a fuel. At the time of Abraham Darby I, 1678 - 1717, iron produced from coke fuel was only good for casting directly into moulds; it was not at first suitable for conversion into wrought iron and its use spread slowly.

Abraham Darby I died in 1717 leaving a son, also named Abraham, who was only six years old. The ironworks was operated by a series of managers with the second Abraham and his sisters only retaining a small share. When he was 17, Abraham Darby II began helping with the running of the ironworks. By 1738 he had become a full partner in the works. It was Abraham Darby II who finally perfected the smelting of iron using coke where the quality of iron produced could be converted into wrought iron. Blast furnaces, fineries, chaferies and slitting mills needed lots of mechanical power for operating bellows, trip hammers and slitting machinery. As the amount of power obtained from water was finite, the extent to which an iron-processing site could grow was severely limited. If there were blast furnaces on a site, the available water power would be used to drive a wheel that operated the bellows for the air charge. This left little or no spare capacity for the operation of hammers or any other mechanical device. Moreover, a blast furnace had to be operated continuously. Once it was taken out of blast it would not be fired again until a continuous water supply for the wheel could be assured.

Blast furnaces, forges and slitting mills were often located separately, each exploiting a local water resource. The problem was aggravated by seasonal fluctuations in the water supply. In some areas even a minor drought brought about cessation of operations. Typically, a blast furnace would only operate for about three-quarters of the year with the dry months being periods for maintenance. The problem of continuing the water supply was alleviated where a Newcomen atmospheric steam engine was used to pump water, which had passed a water wheel, back to a holding reservoir for recycling.

This partly solved the problem of continuance of water power but could not increase the capacity of the site.

A Devon man, Thomas Newcomen invented the atmospheric engine, in 1712 and the first example was erected at Dudley in an area soon to become known as "The Black Country." Several ironmasters had tried to use the Newcomen engine to provide furnace air blast but the erratic operation of this early steam engine could not provide the continuity of blast that was required. The attraction was that if a steam engine could be used to provide the air blast to a furnace, then the water wheel would be free to provide mechanical power for other devices. This meant that several processes could be brought together on one site, eliminating the transport costs between them. Moreover, more furnaces could be operated than would be possible using any available water resource. The idea of using the newly invented steam engine for providing power in an iron foundry would have had enormous appeal to an ironmaster but the operating costs of the Newcomen engine were high and involved the additional burden of transporting large amounts of fuel to the site, which abrogated any possible advantage.

THE IRONMASTER

There is a portrait of John Wilkinson in the Museum of Iron at Ironbridge that reveals to us a rather lugubrious man in his later years. What appears to be a scar shows beneath his left eye and his lips are slightly pouted as if he had been an impatient sitter. The expression in his eyes confirms his impatience and he appears to be staring vacantly as if his mind was elsewhere. Was he thinking of one of his projects, or busily working out a detail for some new plan while he sat for his portrait? This would be typical as one of his sayings was: "more is done by scheming than by working". His complexion is ruddy – perhaps due largely to an outdoor life of travel – necessary if he was to keep effective control of his several iron works and other projects. The redness in his cheeks hardly extends to his rather large nose, indicating that any use of alcohol would have been moderate. The peruke that covers his head, the white cravat at his throat and the high-collared coat complete the picture of a prosperous eighteenth century ironmaster.

John Wilkinson's prospects improved when he married. John married twice during his lifetime and seems to have been fortunate in his choice of wife on both occasions. Marriage in the eighteenth century amongst the merchant class was also a business partnership where one or other of the spouses could bring additional wealth, producing an amalgamation of fortunes usually administered by the husband. An analogy can be drawn with the coming together of two businesses: a business that is under-performing might be transformed into profit by an injection of new capital; conversely, a business that is failing because of its inherent hopelessness, or bad management, can easily drag down a more affluent partner. So it was with eighteenth century marriage. A profligate husband could easily reduce the fortune of the heiress he married. If, however, the joining of two fortunes led to a successful enterprise, both partners would benefit: they would become elevated in social status and both would enjoy increased wealth.

In 1755, John married Anne Maudsley, of Rigmadden Hall near Kirby Lonsdale, and soon produced a daughter, Mary, named after his sister. The family, along with brother William, moved to Bersham where Isaac Wilkinson was operating the ironworks and soon after, on November 17th, Anne died. Their daughter, Mary, was placed into the care of foster parents and after she grew up, she died in child-birth leaving John without an heir. When his wife died, John threw himself into his work and the year 1758 found him in charge at the New Willey ironworks, Broseley, in Shropshire, not far from Coalbrookdale and the Darby's. This is the first time he is referred to as an ironmaster, as he alone of twelve partners had any practical experience of iron making and he had sole charge of the works. Broseley is to the south of the River Severn opposite the Iron Bridge. Records show there had been a blast furnace for the production of iron at Willey, near Broseley since 1620. John Wilkinson, with a twelfth share in the New Willey works, bought a house in Broseley.

It was at New Willey Ironworks where John Wilkinson began introducing the ideas and techniques that were to earn him the sobriquet "Iron Mad Wilkinson." This was a busy period for iron making as the "Seven Years War" was provoking a demand for guns. This war with France began in 1756 and lasted until 1763. During these years, the policy of William Pitt not only restored, but expanded, the earlier empires of Elizabeth and Cromwell. In 1763 John Wilkinson married his second wife - Mary Lee of Wroxeter. She, too, seems to have brought money to the marriage for John, with his brother William, took over the ironworks at Bersham from Isaac, the brothers becoming principals in the business in 1764.

It seems obvious that John was ambitious and fully intended to branch out from New Willey on his own account. This led some of his enemies to put about the idea that he was hiding the true trading figures from the New Willey partners for his own benefit. John was certainly not above creating opportunities for himself, but the partners were shrewd businessmen themselves and it is extremely unlikely that they would be taken in by dishonesty. That the New Willey partners were satisfied with John's management is indicated by his relationship with one of them – Edward Blakeway. Mary Lee, John's second wife was Blakeway's sister-in-law and it had been Blakeway who had introduced the couple. Furthermore, in the year 1774, Blakeway introduced John as a Burgess of Wenlock, something he would hardly have done had there been any doubt as to John's integrity. Undoubtedly, it was the money that came with John's second marriage that helped him with the furtherance of his plans for the future.

DISSENTERS IN THE EIGHTEENTH CENTURY

It is not possible to say exactly what John Wilkinson's religious ideals were, nor can it be stated positively that he was a dissenter. His family certainly had Quaker connections and his sympathy lay with the views of Dr. Joseph Priestly, a Unitarian Minister and his brother-in-law. Priestly was ordained a Dissenting minister in 1762. That same year Priestly married Mary Wilkinson, daughter of Isaac Wilkinson. They went on to have one daughter and three sons. Priestley believed the study of history showed that scientific progress depended more on the accumulation of new facts that anyone could discover, than on the theoretical insights of a few men of supposed genius. As a Dissenter, Priestley preferred facts rather than hypothesis in science, which was consistent with his religious conviction that prejudice and dogma of any sort presented obstacles to individual inquiry and private judgment. In August 1, 1774 he obtained a colourless gas by heating red mercuric oxide. Finding that a candle would burn and that a mouse would thrive in this gas, he called it *dephlogisticated air*, believing that ordinary air became saturated with *phlogiston* once it could no longer support life or, more importantly, combustion. He had, in fact, become the first to identify oxygen.

John was a dealer in armaments and, later in his life, the father of three illegitimate children, so it has been considered curious that he is identified with the Society of Friends (Quakers) at all. These facts would certainly preclude a person from association with present-day Quakers, but it is by no means certain that this would have been the case in the eighteenth century. Although all the evidence we can gather today indicating he had Quaker leanings is circumstantial, the same can be said to the contrary. Quakers were certainly heavily engaged in arms production at the time, a fact that cannot be denied as it is well documented.

The present day Society of Friends do not admit to John Wilkinson having been a Quaker because of his arms dealing and the facts of his illegitimate children. There seem to be no traces of his name in the Society's records, or of his expulsion if he had been one. However, events in John Wilkinson's affairs concerning his family, social and business life indicate a very strong association with Quakers and other dissenting religious groups.

For instance, in 1718, Charles Lloyd had founded the Bersham iron works. Lloyd was a Quaker whose friendship with Abraham Darby, also a Quaker, led to the Bersham furnace being used to smelt iron, using coke as a fuel. The works were taken over by John Hawking, a son-in-law of Darby. Hawking's wife ran it after her husband's death until the lease was taken over by Isaac Wilkinson in 1753. Years later, when Isaac Wilkinson retired from business, he went to live at Bristol where there was a large Quaker population.

John's involvement with gun making was an important part of the work at Bersham. The manufacture of armaments was a substantial and profitable part of the iron trade in the eighteenth century. It is unlikely that an ironmaster of any ambition would, or could, ignore the considerable profits to be made. An iron making concern that had no involvement with arms manufacture would have difficulty rising to a significant position in the industry. In the mid-eighteenth century, the ironworks at Coalbrookdale were amongst the most important in England and there is evidence that guns were made there during the Seven Years War and up to about 1790. The Darby's and other prominent Quaker families dominated this area. When subscribers were listed for the construction project that was to build the world's first iron bridge across the River Severn in Coalbrookdale, the name of John Wilkinson appeared second only to that of Abraham Darby III. The Iron Bridge opened in 1779 and it is obvious John was far from being persona-non-grata so far as Quakers were concerned in that year.

The foremost artillery expert in Europe in the eighteenth century was also a Quaker – Benjamin Robins was born at Bath in 1707. In 1742 he published a book on gunnery stating, amongst other things, the advantages of rifling in gun barrels. The following year he read a paper before the Royal Society. The paper was entitled: "New Principles of Gunnery", and pointed out that the powder charge of guns commonly used was generally too great for the projectile and did not increase the range of the shot. Perhaps Quakers in the eighteenth century took a more pragmatic view, regarding the manufacture of armaments, than their counterparts today. What seems to be the case is that gun founding certainly went on in iron works owned and controlled by Quaker families. If conditions of membership to the Society of Friends had been interpreted in the eighteenth century as today, then John certainly would not have been allowed association with them - but clearly involvement in arms manufacture was not deemed a barrier at the time and the circumstantial evidence indicates that the Wilkinson's could have been Quakers.

The educational establishments of the day were barred to Dissenters as the grammar schools and universities required conformance to the Thirty-Nine Articles of the established Church (originally drawn up in the reign of Elizabeth 1st). The Toleration Act, introduced in the reign of William and Mary, provided some freedom of worship for Protestant Dissenters but did not give them free access to the educational establishments. Unitarians and papists were excluded from the benefits of the Act. All Dissenters were excluded from parliamentary careers, civil careers and military office. Dissenters were educated in their own schools, which were known as academies. The dissenting academies provided tuition in mathematics, science and foreign languages - a type of education particularly suited to business. The education received by Dissenters helped to establish the conditions for the Industrial Revolution as well as providing the entrepreneurs and inventors who pioneered it

In John Wilkinson's day, within living memory there had been several attempts at removing Protestant kings from the English throne. The Jacobite rebellion of 1745 was still fresh in the minds of everyone, as was the earlier Jacobite revolution of 1715. Although British Catholics made these attempts, suspicion and distrust naturally fell on all dissenting groups. In the period 1779 - 1784 there were invasion scares, and these, coupled with ignominious defeat in America, made the government understandably nervous. Industrial riots and religious disturbances would occur at the slightest provocation. The cotton industry was particularly affected by the war with America and, in the autumn of 1779, large mobs attacked buildings and smashed machines in five Lancashire towns. In Chorley, a mob of 2000 who were attacking a mill were repulsed with two killed and eight wounded. This inflamed the mob, which returned the next day, this time 8000 strong, having been reinforced by colliers, and destroyed the machinery. In 1789 the French Revolution began with the ideals of the revolutionaries being admired by intellectuals such as Joseph Priestly and other social reformers in England - a situation that made a feeble government even more jumpy.

It is not surprising that Dissenters were attracted to the ideals of the French Revolution. It had long been considered that the lot of the French Huguenot (Protestant) had been far worse than that of the

English Dissenter. Suddenly, in the revolution of 1789, the situation was reversed. Religious equality now flourished in France while in England the "Test" and "Corporation" Acts deprived Dissenters of full citizenship. By law, Unitarians were not even tolerated. In 1790, Priestly stated that he regretted finding himself on the opposite side of the argument to Edmund Burke whose "Reflections on the French Revolution" supported the French court.

At first, the French Revolution was not associated with tyranny and sudden, brutal death. Anne Holt, in her book on the life of Joseph Priestly put it this way: "When the French Revolution broke out, it was generally hailed as the dawning of a brighter day. Corruption, tyranny and war were now about to disappear, and the reign of universal peace and brotherhood would begin." As a Unitarian, Joseph Priestly believed that although Jesus Christ was a religious teacher of great merit, he was not a deity. Unitarian emphasis was on God as the Almighty and they believed strongly in The Brotherhood of Man, a point of view that caused great offence to the established Church of the day.

John seems to have been in full agreement with the principles held by Dr Joseph Priestley; that people should be able to speak openly, be free from religious persecution and able to explore new ideas without prejudice. Radical political thought in the eighteenth century expounded the aggrandisement of the people relative to the aristocracy, a point of view shared by the population of America and which had encouraged the revolution in France. Not surprisingly, the established authorities in England, the Church, and those with vast lands, were against such notions, as were a large section of the population who mistrusted change and relied on the old order to provide stability. It was never a difficult job to fire up the crowd against those who had, or were suspected of having, radical views.

Priestly fell foul of the mob during the Birmingham Riots of 1791 when a mob, incensed by the support by Unitarians for the ideals of the French Revolution, attacked and burned his house and those of other prominent dissenters. In all, two Unitarian meeting houses and one belonging to the Baptists, along with several shops and houses of Dissenters were burned before order was restored. It was thought that the authorities, who were slow to respond to the riots, were in agreement with the mob. Priestly, who was lucky to escape with his life, was unable to return to Birmingham and, with money from his brother-in-law, John Wilkinson, later, in 1794 migrated to America taking his family with him. These political ideals must have affected John's attitude to his work force and, although he would have extracted every ounce of effort out of them, there is evidence that his workers were looked after, some being given pensions when too old or infirm to work – something almost unheard of at the time. We can deduce, then, that although there is no positive record of John Wilkinson's actual political philosophy, by aligning himself with the views of Joseph Priestly it is reasonable to assume where his sympathies lay.

ENGINES OF MORTALITY

Although much business was to be had gun founding, there were problems too. In the period approaching the American War of Independence (1776-1783), the government of Britain was concerned about the quality of ordnance, particularly at sea. Ordnance was "proofed" by loading the barrel with a triple gunpowder charge then firing it from a safe distance to see if it disintegrated. Guns were regularly failing their proof tests at Woolwich Arsenal and those that did pass often burst in service causing injury and death to sailors and damage to naval vessels. The method used for manufacturing these "engines of mortality" as they were termed had not changed very much since 1540.

A gun would be cast from the blast furnace directly into a loam mould having a core for the establishment of the bore. On cooling, the casting would have to be of uniform quality, free from cavities and loam (used in the mould). As the cast gun cooled any impurities from slag in the blast furnace and stress around the cored hole, which cooled the metal there at a different rate from the bulk of the casting, would induce weaknesses that often meant failure when the gun was fired. After removal from the mould the core was extracted and the bore would be machined with a rotary cutter. This operation required great precision to ensure that the bore was exactly central and the right size to take the projectile. The early method of boring guns was to mount the gun, bore downwards, on a vertical carriage. Below the carriage was the boring bar, vertically arranged and having a series of cutters on top, which was rotated by a horse, or perhaps by a waterwheel. As the boring bar rotated, the gun, secured in the frame, would be lowered so that the cutters entered the bore to cut it. This method, although successful with brass guns, was not very satisfactory with cast iron, which was much harder.

Anyone with the money could set up to supply guns to the navy. One Member of Parliament, Anthony Bacon, wanted to supply the Board of Ordnance with guns. Bacon was a merchant with the right contacts but who did not have the skills necessary for gun founding and so he began to look around for a sub-contractor who would do the work. Later, he intended to set up his own gun-foundry, but in 1773 he made contact with John Wilkinson who had inherited the gun-making skills of his father. At this period John and his brother

William were manufacturing guns by the standard method with a cored bore but with greater attention to quality control and with improved boring equipment. When Bacon approached John Wilkinson with the objective of Wilkinson supplying guns through him to the Board of Ordnance, John came up with a much better method of manufacture. Such was the effectiveness of this new method that the Board of Ordnance cancelled all orders for guns using the former method and only accepted guns made by Wilkinson's method.

There were several elements to this new process. Rather than cast the guns directly from the blast furnace, John used iron that was re-melted in a reverberatory furnace. In a reverberatory furnace the iron was placed separately from the fuel. Because the fuel was separate from the iron it did not need to have the purity required for smelting so ordinary coal was used straight from the pit. Heat from the furnace was reflected off the roof of the reverberatory furnace to be concentrated onto the iron, which melted. Any impurities in the iron would be driven off thereby improving its quality. Scrap iron could be introduced with pig iron, or iron from charcoal blast furnaces could be mixed with coke-made iron. Whatever the source of iron, the important thing was that quality could be controlled and uniformity introduced. This re-melted iron was poured into the gun casting boxes without a core so that the gun was solid with no bore. John pioneered the use of casting boxes with green sand for the mould rather than loam. These boxes and the sand could be reused making the process more cost-effective.

The next stage in the process was to bore out the gun from the solid. By casting the gun with much improved quality iron, and boring from solid, a much better gun was produced. This method was used for making brass guns. Although it was relatively easy to drill brass from solid, it was quite another matter to try to drill poor quality cast iron. Wilkinson's quality control gave a more malleable casting, which made it practical to use a drill. The final part of the process was the final machining to size of the gun bore. To do this, John developed a new boring machine. The gun was mounted on a horizontal frame and secured firmly. As the boring bar containing the cutters rotated, it was moved into the bore of the gun. Drive to the boring bar was provided by a water wheel, which was more reliable and stable than horse power.

This new method provided an extremely accurate bore and the machine was later to be adapted so that the cylinders of steam engines ordered by James Watt could be machined to Watt's exacting standards.

Bacon paid for the manufacture of a gun by this new method and had it tested at Woolwich Arsenal. The gun was made at Broseley and easily passed its proof test. Subsequent guns made by Wilkinson consistently passed at proof and the Board of Ordnance immediately cancelled orders for guns from other manufacturers that were made by the old-fashioned method. Wilkinson applied for a patent for his "New Method of Casting and Boring Iron Guns Or Cannon." This caused other gun-founders to complain that they could not make guns without infringing Wilkinson's patent. The Board of Ordnance suggested that if another gun-founder used Wilkinson's process then Wilkinson could sue, but the Board's solicitor would support the plaintiff. Obviously, the Board was concerned that, should the control of gun-founding be with just one person, there would be problems with supply and cost. John Wilkinson did not pursue his patent application and it lapsed on the 16th June 1779.

This brings us to a circumstance that is extraordinary to us today, but which was not considered unusual in the eighteenth century - a visit to Bersham, in 1775, by Marchant de Houliere, a Frenchman whose declared task was to report on English manufacture of cannon as French cannon was acknowledged to be inferior. Remember that this was a time when Britain was barely at peace with France, (although not actually at war) yet here was a brigadier in the French army moving freely about the country and reporting on English methods of gun manufacture! Moreover, as a direct result of Marchant de Houliere's visit, the very next year William Wilkinson went over to France and helped set up a gun-making foundry, on an island in the Loire near Nantes, using techniques developed at Bersham. Perhaps this was the Wilkinson's way of getting their revenge for the loss of the patent rights for their own gun-making process.

John, meanwhile, was working on another project for France - the supply of forty miles of cast-iron pipes for the Paris Water Company of "Perrier". Representatives of Perrier, the water engineer for Paris, had come to England to see John Wilkinson at his foundries and ordered the pipes, which were improvements on earlier ones as these had been bored from wood. The pipes were openly shipped in one of Wilkinson's ships, the "Mary" in accordance with passports from both the English and French governments. The Paris scheme was to bring water from the Seine into the city to be discharged from public fountains or into private homes on payment of a subscription. This water was previously drawn directly from the river downstream of the main sewer outlets! The purpose of Perrier's scheme was to bring water into Paris from the river above the city.

Cast iron pipes, whatever the intended use, have a marked similarity to gun barrels and it is not surprising that accusations of gun running began to be heard. John was a successful ironmaster and a major supplier of guns. He must have had some powerful enemies, particularly amongst the less proficient of gun makers who had found their lucrative trade curtailed due to the superior quality of the Wilkinson guns. It would have been easy to spread rumours, but the lack of any hint of prosecution against Wilkinson seems to testify to his innocence. It is reasonable to suppose that the authorities in the eighteenth century would have made what would be an easy and obvious check of the cargoes in the Wilkinson ships.

BORING STEAM ENGINE CYLINDERS

At the end of the war with America, the orders for ordnance dried up. This was a serious problem for some foundries, but John had an idea that turned the situation around for him and introduced a new and exciting venture, which helped transform the way, the world worked. Steam engines (or fire engines as they were called at the time) had been around from 1712 when Thomas Newcomen, erected the first efficient "atmospheric" engine at Dudley in Staffordshire. The working cylinder of an early Newcomen atmospheric engine was cast in bronze. It was not possible to produce a cylinder with an accurate, round bore as there was no known method of machining it; roundness of a cylinder bore was totally reliant on the skill of the brass-founder.

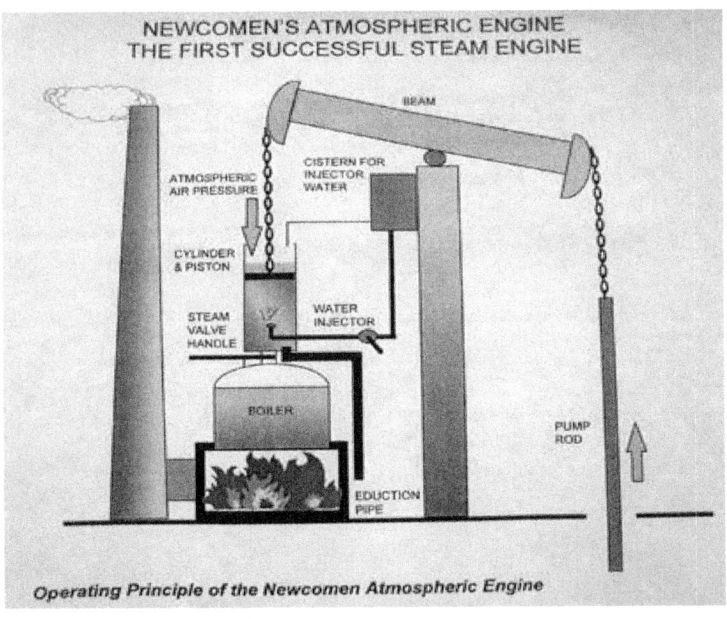

Operating Principle of the Newcomen Atmospheric Engine

Newcomen's engine used atmospheric pressure to drive a piston down a cylinder to pull down a rocking beam to which a pump rod was suspended at the opposite end to the piston. Steam was introduced into the cylinder as the piston was pulled up the bore by the weight of the pump rods hanging from the end of a wooden beam, the piston being suspended by a chain at the cylinder end. Cold water was then injected below the piston to rapidly cool the steam to create the vacuum. This would drive the piston down the bore of the cylinder and raise the pump rods at the other end of the beam. Using this machine, water could then be raised by the attached pump. A piston would be in two parts, one above the other, with hemp rope packed between to provide some sort of seal. Even so, a piston was only considered to be a good fit if nothing larger than a copper penny could be pushed between it and the bore of the cylinder. To make the piston air tight, water was continually poured into the top of it to maintain some sort of seal. Much of this water would be drawn by vacuum into the cylinder on the power stroke, but as this helped condense the steam it was not too much of a problem provided the water seal was adequately maintained.

When James Watt invented the separate condenser, it would be effective only if the piston could properly seal the working cylinder. Watt's invention condensed the steam to produce vacuum in a separate vessel meaning that the working cylinder could remain hot, instead of being alternately heated and cooled as with Newcomen's machine. Vacuum would still power the piston but great thermal savings were made, as the power of the steam was not lost by entering a working cylinder made cool by the injection water of the previous stroke. On the power stroke the hot steam was drawn into the separate cold condenser vessel thus producing the required vacuum and using much less steam with a greater economy of fuel. A water seal over the piston was no use because the water would have cooled the working cylinder, partly condensing the steam within. The whole objective of Watt's engine was to keep the working cylinder hot and the separate condenser cold. Clearly, this required an efficient mechanical seal between the piston and the cylinder bore. Unless a cast iron cylinder could be made with an accurate round bore, Watt's engine would be no more efficient than the Newcomen engine, in fact it would not work at all.

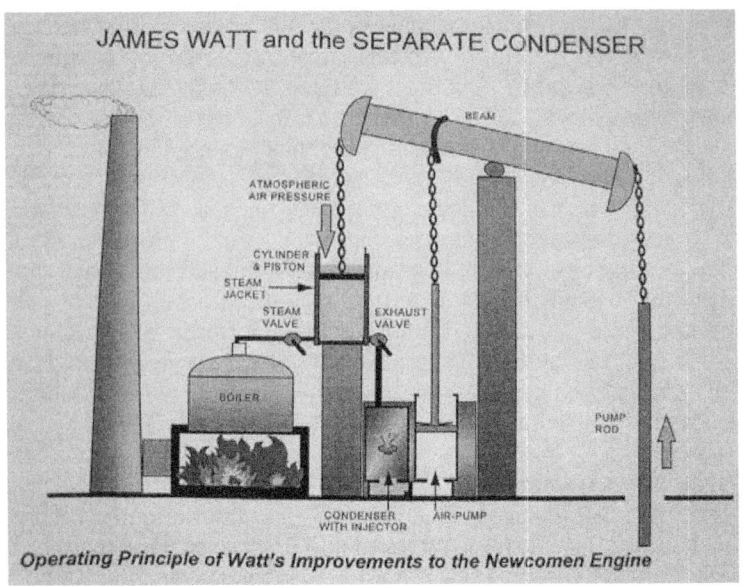
Operating Principle of Watt's Improvements to the Newcomen Engine

The first Watt engines were provided with a reasonably round bore by the rather laborious method of smoothing the bore with abrasive material and working the engine with the piston packed with paper, sealed with horse of cow dung. This was clearly a major stumbling block to the proper operation of the engine and so Watt's partner, Matthew Boulton, approached the man he had heard was one of the best ironmasters in England, John Wilkinson, and asked him to produce an engine cylinder with a true, round bore. Watt had recently entered into partnership with Matthew Boulton, at Soho in Birmingham.

Matthew Boulton was a manufacturer of buttons and wanted to use a steam engine to operate his machinery. Seeing the potential of Watt's idea of the separate condenser, he provided the necessary facility for experimentation.

John cast a cylinder and then adapted his cannon-boring machine so that he could machine it out, providing a round bore, which permitted a good seal with the piston. Before Wilkinson's machine, there had been severe problems associated with boring steam engine cylinders. The cylinders of a Newcomen engine would be cast in brass or bronze, probably in a bell foundry, as the techniques used in these establishments were better suited to casting a cylinder.

After casting, a brass cylinder would be scraped manually to obtain a reasonably round bore. Cast iron, on the other hand, being much harder, was too difficult a material to work by hand and required special cutting machinery for boring it out.

Early boring mills were adaptations of equipment designed for boring wooden pipes. A cylinder would be strapped down to a wheeled carriage. A waterwheel provided the drive for the rotation of a boring bar of a length corresponding to the length of the cylinder to be bored. With this arrangement it was impossible to move the boring bar axially, which is why the wheeled carriage was used. The cutting head was mounted on the end of the boring bar and the wheeled carriage was moved into the cutters, drawn by a chain and windlass. Any inaccuracy in the alignment or profile of the rails along which the carriage was drawn would be reproduced in the cylinder bore. Moreover, because the boring bar was only supported at one end (cantilevered) the cutting end would deflect producing a distorted bore. John Smeaton (1724-1792) constructed an improved boring mill for machining Newcomen engine cylinders, but this was only a more accurate version of the standard boring mill and did not overcome the inherent inaccuracies of the design. John Wilkinson identified the two principle problems with the early boring mill and solved them. The tendency of a cantilevered boring bar to deflect was overcome by supporting the boring bar at each end of the cylinder. Fixing the cylinder so that it could not move while it was being bored eliminated inaccuracy in the cylinder alignment. Of course, the cutting head had to advance through the cylinder, and John managed this by making the cutting head a sliding fit along the boring bar. The boring bar was hollow, with slots on the outside to the inner bore.

A driving dog was installed in the cutting head and through the slots. When the boring bar turned, the driving dog caused the cutting head to rotate with it. A push-rod in the hollow bar pushed against the driving dog to feed the cutting head along the bar and through the cylinder.

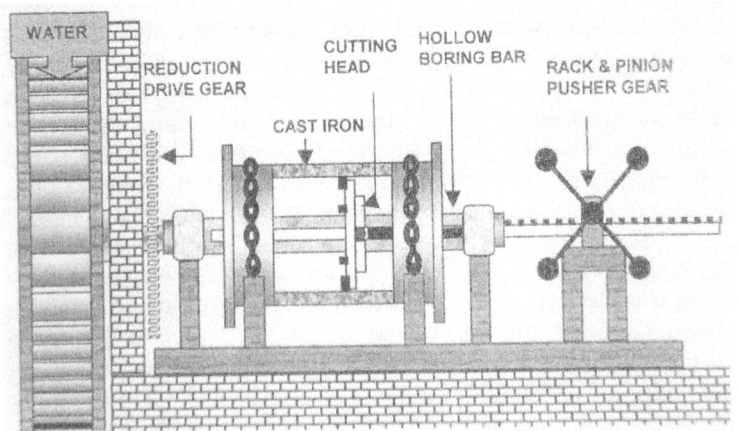

Wilkinson's Boring Machine

The importance of John's design cannot be over-stated. The cylinder was fixed and could not move. The boring bar was secure at each end and could rotate without deflecting. The cutting head, which turned with the boring bar, could only move along the axis of the bar. Providing he aligned properly the boring bar with the centre of the cylinder, Wilkinson could accomplish accuracy hitherto undreamed of. Without this accuracy, cylinders good enough for the double-acting steam engine would not have been possible to produce, and the efficiency of single-acting engines would have remained as for Newcomen engines. With only slight modifications, such as replacing the inner push-bar with a machined screw, Wilkinson's method of operation, and design of boring bar, was used until the end of the steam age in the 1970's.

The material used for cutting tools was steel made by the cementation process, which produced what was commonly known as blister steel due to its blistered surface. Much of this steel was imported from Sweden and Russia where the cementation process had been perfected. Cementation converted the wrought iron into steel by carbonisation to give a carbon content of around 1.0%. Wrought iron bars were placed in a furnace covered with charcoal and fired at high temperature (900oC) for about a week. The grade of steel produced depended on the length of time spent at this temperature. This very expensive process is what gave the wrought iron bars their blistered appearance.

The conversion of five hundred pounds of iron into steel using the earlier method required fifty tons of charcoal. By the eighteenth century, steel produced by the cementation process was being made using coal as a fuel which substantially reduced its cost, although it was much more expensive than iron. Further heat treatment and forging converted the wrought iron to steel, which was tempered to give sufficient hardness for making the cutting tools. After 1742 the process, invented in this year by Benjamin Huntsman, could make cutting tools but did not come into general use until about 1770. Huntsman used a clay crucible to contain Swedish blister steel and flux in a furnace. The high temperature in the furnace would drive of any impurities and the molten steel was then poured into a mould. This very hard steel is likely to be the type of cutting tool material that Wilkinson would have used.

JOHN WILKINSON'S STEAM ENGINES

The first of James Watt's new steam engine was the experimental Kinneal engine, which had been re-erected in Matthew Boulton's factory at Soho, Birmingham. This engine had not been a great success, being the first steam engine to be built using a separate (surface) condenser and there were problems with sealing the piston in the cylinder. It must, however, have made an impression on John as in 1775 he ordered a blowing engine to provide the blast for his furnaces at the New Willey works, near Broseley. This was the first time the new design of boring bar would be used.

It can be seen that the Watt engine, still simple by modern standards, was much more complex than the Newcomen engine. As well as a steam valve, an exhaust valve was needed. Both valves were operated automatically by a rod suspended from the beam. Also there was the separate condenser and air pump. A Watt engine was three times more efficient than a Newcomen engine and therefore only used one-third the fuel for the same work. The blowing engine was constructed in Wilkinson's own workshops and Watt declared: "the cylinder and the fitting of the piston are beyond my most sanguine hopes. It seems to be truth itself"

Wilkinson's engine had a bore of 38" (965mm) and was put to work about March 1776. Although the engine worked, there must have been teething problems and it is expected that Wilkinson, being a practical man, would have dealt with these as they arose. In August, 1779 he wrote to Watt complaining about the problems he had encountered in operating what was, after all, a pioneer engine. Being a shrewd businessman, John had heard of new design improvements to engines subsequently built by Boulton and Watt and wanted these applied to the blowing engine. Watt wrote back explaining that he would have preferred to have experimented with the engine further before building it for commercial use, but business pressures and demand for results by his partner, Matthew Boulton, had led him to erect the engine before he was entirely satisfied with the working principle. Watt was fortunate that this early engine had been built and operated by a practical man like John Wilkinson. A less able purchaser would have had great difficulty making it work. John's complaint had some useful effect, however, as new valves were fitted to the blowing engine and it may be presumed that the engine worked satisfactorily afterwards.

The New Willey (Broseley) engine operated a blowing cylinder rather than the cam drive to a series of bellows as was the practice with a waterwheel drive. The working cylinder was 38 inches (965mm) diameter and the piston stroke was eight feet (2.4 metres). The air (blowing) cylinder had a diameter of 72 inches (1828mm) with a seven-foot (2.1 metres) stroke. It was the first time that a steam engine had provided the means of supplying air to a blast furnace. This very first iron-works beam engine lifted a piston in a cylinder, which forced air into the tuyere of a blast furnace. On the down stroke the cylinder was recharged with air through flap valves in the piston. This meant there would have been a pause in the draught on each return stroke. As a blast furnace required a constant supply of air, a means of storing some of the air charge, to be released on the up-stroke of the engine, was required. John's solution was a simple accumulator, the idea for which was most probably based upon his father's system of 1757, which had provided the remote air blast at Bersham using water displacement.

An open-topped cistern was constructed of brickwork to contain water. Within the cistern was an inverted chamber with the top closed off and loaded with further brickwork (to prevent the top blowing off under air pressure). Two pipes were connected to the inverted chamber – one communicating with the air cylinder and the other with the tuyere of the blast furnace. A one-way valve in the pipe from the air cylinder would open on the air stroke and close on the return stroke. As air entered the inverted chamber, water was pushed down while rising in the outer chamber. Residual air passed along the supply pipe to the tuyere. Water would rise in the outer cistern disproportionately to that inside the inverted chamber. On the return stroke, with no air coming from the air cylinder, the water in the inverted chamber would rise, due to the disproportionate weight of water in the outer cistern, displacing the air above so that the valve in the air supply pipe from the blowing cylinder would close, directing the displaced air into the tuyere pipe. This arrangement provided a continuous draught, though not at continuous pressure. Later, because of the accuracy provided by Wilkinson's boring machine, Watt was able to develop the double-acting engine where power was provided in both directions allowing a continuous pumping action in an air cylinder.

Wilkinson's ingenuity produced a similar effect at a time when only a single acting engine was available.

Another interesting steam engine, designed by Watt, but known to have been built by John Wilkinson at the New Willey works, was popularly called the "Topsey-Turvey" engine. This engine dispensed with the familiar beam and the working cylinder was inverted directly over a water pump to which it was connected by the piston rod. The intended use of the Topsey-Turvey engine was to pump water to one of the waterwheels that provided the power for boring cannon. Watt had taken a long time to develop the separate condenser because his early experiments had been with engines having inverted cylinders that worked directly from the piston rod. Difficulties with this design held him back until he gave in and applied the beam, as in a Newcomen engine. It seems that the idea for the design persisted and it is not difficult to see where the attraction lay.

Wilkinson, too, must have been smitten as he actually constructed this engine for use in his own works. Other engineers of the time, notably Bull, were to pursue the same idea. An inverted cylinder dispensing with the beam, simplifying the design and lowering construction costs. At this time beams were of wood and Watt, in common with other engine builders, had agents scouring the country for suitable timber. He was competing with every other industry from house building to ship building. Timber of substantial size could only be obtained in the face of stiff competition and at exorbitant prices. With an inverted engine, the piston would be connected directly to the driven component, with a saving of transmission parts and mechanical joints – this was the idea, but reality intervened. Gravity meant that a piston, and its attached components, would be weighted downwards contrary to the power stroke that was induced by vacuum above the piston, directing the force upwards. This would result in a loss of power, as the whole of the weight would have to be overcome by the working cylinder with no mechanical advantage through the leverage of a beam. With an inverted cylinder, a piston lid, with stuffing gland, would have been needed to prevent the piston, and therefore the whole assembly, falling out of the cylinder. There must have been some problems with the return stroke. Beam engines had weights attached to their beams above the working cylinder to counterbalance the weight of pump rods at the other end – this was not possible with an inverted engine. The opening of the steam valve above the piston would have caused the piston to drop, imposing great strain on any restraints as well as the working components. If there was a system of counterbalancing the pumping assembly, it would have been complex and more difficult to assemble than with a simple beam engine. Further design problems would arise from the arrangement for driving the valve gear and the air pump. On a beam engine these items were simply operated by rods suspended from the beam. With an inverted engine, the operating equipment would have had to be driven from the piston rod, imposing further complications and more difficult maintenance.

John Wilkinson seems to have had an arrangement with Boulton and Watt regarding the payment of premiums for operating engines upon Watt's principles. Watt's patent for the separate condenser would not expire until 1800. Users of this new technology had to pay one-third of the savings they were making over the operating costs of an equivalent Newcomen engine. As a Watt engine only consumed one third of the fuel that a corresponding Newcomen engine burned, this represented a good bargain for the owner of the engine. Because Wilkinson was of considerable help in building and solving manufacturing problems with these early engines, the terms for payment of premiums was fairly relaxed. Later, when Boulton and Watt were producing castings in their own foundry, and when brother William was causing trouble for John, the relationship seemed to sour.

Whether John deliberately infringed Watt's patent by building engines on his (Watt's) principles for his own use is not clear; what is known is that there were accusations of patent infringement and litigation was later directed at John who regarded himself as being an equal to Watt himself when it came to steam engine development. This point of view was not unreasonable as Wilkinson built the first Watt engines in his own works, ironed out the operating and design problems, and developed the means of ensuring that the critical mechanical parts were made to the necessary accuracy.

John built further single-acting engines at Wilson house (1778), Bradley Ironworks in Staffordshire (1779), Snedshill Ironworks, Shropshire (1780) and at Brymbo, North Wales, in 1796. In 1782 John installed one of Watt's new rotative engines at Bradley iron works. It was a single-acting engine and had the sun-and-planet system of drive to a flywheel, the shaft of which was connected to a cam that operated a forge hammer. The rotative engine was an important development in steam engine design as it meant that rotating machinery could be driven by steam rather than have to rely on a water wheel with its associated power supply problems. What is surprising, having regard for Wilkinson's dedication to the universal use of iron, is that iron does not seem to have been used for making an engine beam until very late in the century. There is a record of a Boulton and Watt blowing engine with an iron beam at Carron ironworks, Scotland in 1802. All the engines for Wilkinson seem to have had wooden beams, but it must be remembered that the steam engine as we know it was in its infancy in Wilkinson's day and it would have been more practical to provide an engine with a shock-absorbing wooden beam than cast iron which, at this time, was still an experimental material in engineering. Even as late as 1793, Watt's rotative engines still had wooden beams.

THE TRIAL

At a place called Apley Wharf near New Willey on the River Severn, Monday 9th July 1787, to the salute from a pair of 32 pounder cannon, the world's first iron boat "The Trial" was launched. A huge crowd had gathered expecting to see its innovator, "Iron Mad" Wilkinson confounded as the boat sank – but it floated and the fickle crowd roared its approval. A newspaper report of the time stated that the boat was made of English Iron and was 70 feet long by 6 feet 8.5" wide with a draught of eight or nine inches.

Throughout the history of mankind there are many examples of those who have invested time, money and effort into a project that seemed hopeless to everyone else. So it was with John Wilkinson and his iron boat. With the cheers of the crowd ringing in his ears, perhaps John would have been thinking of the days when he worked with his father at Wilson House and of the iron barge that Isaac might have built to transport peat along the cuts in the diggings? Maybe he had made a smaller version of the boat and tried it secretly in a tub of water before embarking on the full-scale project. It is unlikely that he would have been "mad" enough to commit a large amount of money and effort unless he knew that he would succeed. We have no way of knowing, but we can surmise that John would have been elated when the vessel took to the water and rocked gently on the surface.

The ability to transport raw materials to an ironworks, then to ship out the finished product was of paramount importance to an ironmaster. Roads were mostly rough and impassable in bad weather. The easiest way to transport goods in bulk was by water, which is why medieval towns and cities were built on a waterway such as a river or where the geography of a sea shore permitted the construction of a safe harbour. In Wilkinson's day the only other reliable form of transport overland was still by packhorse. Wagons would only be used for relatively short haul journeys and could never be used on roads rendered to mud by the weather and the passage of horses. This prompted the beginning of the canal building era, with the first canal between St. Helens and Liverpool being opened in 1757.

Another canal, built in 1759 by the Duke of Bridgewater, linked his coal mines at Worseley to his mills in Manchester. Canals were particularly good for transporting heavy materials such as coal, iron and limestone as well as manufactured goods. By the end of the century a network of canals had spread through the Midlands and the North of England. Ironmasters, with heavy raw materials and finished goods to move, had to concern themselves with the problems of transport and it is not surprising that John Wilkinson turned his attention to the building of a boat in his preferred material – iron. At the time this was a completely novel notion, as everyone knew that a lump of iron would sink where wood floated. A local blacksmith, hearing of John's iron boat project, contemptuously threw a horse shoe into a trough of water and laughed to scorn the idea of iron being able to float. Prejudice and ignorance aside, though, there were some fairly difficult obstacles to be overcome before a workable iron boat could be constructed. The transportation of goods along the River Severn out of Wilkinson's ironworks at Broseley relied on a type of vessel known as a trow. A trow was a flat-bottomed barge with clinker built sides driven by a square-rigged sail. The Severn trow was generally lighter in construction than those similar vessels that worked the rivers and estuaries. Trows were, of course, built of wood and their lightness of construction was necessary to successfully navigate, with a full load, the shallows and mud banks of the river.

In order for John to construct an iron boat, it too would have to be light enough to provide the shallow draught needed on the river. The main problem was how to make the iron plates of a suitable size and thin enough to keep the weight of the vessel down. In 1787 wrought iron was a new material; it could be rolled and shaped but its laminar structure meant it could not easily be produced in plate thin enough for Wilkinson's purpose. Holes had to be provided as the plates would have had to be riveted or bolted together. Wrought iron could be heated and the holes punched through, but this was a laborious and costly exercise. If plates were made of cast iron, however, holes for rivets could be provided at the casting stage and there would be no need for rolling or forging. The problem was casting iron plates in a section thin enough for the purpose. A newspaper account at the time mentioned that the plates were 5/16" thick. This would certainly have established a practical weight for the vessel, but the casting of plates this thin was a task beyond most iron works of the time. The technical problems would have included distortion of the plates as the castings cooled, and faults in the iron due to impurities in the molten metal as it came from the blast furnace. Faults in iron just 5/16" thick would make such plates useless for boat building purposes. These obstacles would have been seen by John as a challenge in his quest to prove that iron was a constructional material as universal as wood.

Impurities in iron straight from the blast furnace came from residues of fuel and ore that had not been entirely purged out in blast. The technique John used for making cannon was just as good for casting iron plates. By carefully selecting pig iron and scrap, then mixing and re-melting it in a reverberatory furnace, not only could quality be controlled but also any impurities would be removed and the carbon content improved. The resulting iron, being of uniform quality, would mould better and be free from faults caused by impurities. John Wilkinson's special casting expertise meant that he would have been able to cast iron plates of a size, and thin enough, for the hull of "The Trial".

Nothing is known of the way in which "The Trial" was actually constructed. Comparisons with iron plates from a water tank found in John Wilkinson's former house at Broseley, "The Lawns" suggest that the plates were probably lap-jointed and either bolted or riveted together. The plates used in the construction of the water tank are thought to date from the time when John occupied the house. They are of the right thickness and tests have shown that the iron had been re-melted rather than poured straight from a blast furnace.

The place where The "Trial" was constructed is also the subject of some controversy - was it built in the iron works at New Willey away from the launch site or on the riverbank at Apley Wharf. The probability is that it was constructed at or near to the actual launch site. The problems of moving the finished hull of a barge the size of "The Trial" would have been almost impossible at the time. Because of the state of the roads in the 18th century, it was common for industrialists to construct rail or plate ways. Rails were made from wood and it was much easier for a wagon to be moved by horses along a railway than over a rough track. There would have had to have been some sort of rail track from the ironworks at New Willey to the river as the regular and efficient passage of goods could not be assured by any other method. This could have been the way in which a boat might be transported.

The topography around the area, however, mitigates against this due to the tight bends and steepness of such a track. It would have been much easier to transport the iron plates along a rail track and assemble the boat at the launch site.

There is no record of how many iron boats were built by John Wilkinson, or whether he actually used such vessels. It may be that he was content with merely demonstrating the "impossible" by making iron float and for practical purposes continued to use the conventional wooden vessels. One thing is obvious; that once the principle had been demonstrated others would take up the idea, which is what actually happened.

THE IRON BUSINESS

John Wilkinson was one of many ironmasters in the eighteenth century and he was engaged in a very competitive industry. The expansion of iron production began after the tyranny of charcoal as a fuel was broken, and it was not long before the skills of those who were engaged in iron smelting were at a premium. John owned, or had interests in, iron works at New Willey, Hadley and Snedhill - Shropshire, Bradley in Staffordshire, Wilson House at Lindale and Bersham and Brymbo in North Wales.

An eighteenth century iron works was not a very attractive place. There would be a conglomeration of buildings of various forms, all stained with the grimy products of smoke. Huge piles of raw materials were stockpiled – limestone, ore and coke for the blast furnaces, sand for making moulds for casting, and coal for the reverberatory furnaces or for coking. Roads would be thick with dust, mud and the droppings of the dozens of horses that were used for haulage. Slag from the furnaces and scrap iron would lie in piles. Finished goods were stored either in a warehouse or in the works yard. Smoke belched from the furnaces and forges while sulphurous fumes hung heavily in the air. If coke for the furnaces was being prepared from coal, then the fumes from the coking ovens would add to the stink. Continuous noise would come from the hammers that stamped and crushed the iron ore and limestone into pieces to a size suitable for feeding the blast furnace. Other hammers beat the cast iron into wrought iron. Everywhere was noise and dirt that would permeate the district around the iron works for a considerable distance. At night, the sky would glow red with reflected light from the blast furnaces. Every so often a furnace would be "tapped" and the white-hot iron would flow along channels to the pig beds, or be collected into ladles, which were carried by men to the casting moulds where the liquid iron was poured.

John operated the ironworks at Bersham in partnership with his brother, William. As this and the other businesses in which John was concerned developed, William and John began to have differences of opinion that were to end in acrimony. This was perhaps why it was William who went to France, rather than John, to set up an ironworks there for the French. In 1785, William set up and operated a blast furnace at Le Creusot.

The following year, William left Le Creusot and visited Prussia and other countries before returning to England around 1788. He married a widow, Mrs. Elizabeth Kirklees in the January of 1791 and three years later, in 1794, quarrelled with John to the extent that, a year later, Bersham was shut down, the brothers deciding to sell up and divide the proceeds.

The cause of the dispute was John's purchase of the nearby Brymbo estate. Apparently William considered that he should have been included in the deal since he was John's partner at Bersham. There are conflicting accounts about the arguments between the two brothers, some of which must be regarded as being apocryphal. One dramatic account has the two brothers marching on the iron works each at the head of a group of workmen. In the ensuing battle the equipment and machinery of Bersham was said to have been smashed so that it would be useless to the eventual victor. This is most unlikely as both brothers were much to sanguine to destroy capital equipment. The story does, however, hand down to us some of the feelings of bitterness that existed between the brothers. After this the brothers went their separate ways and they never seem to have patched up their differences.

Correspondence from William to other prominent businessmen of the time indicates most of the acrimony and bad feeling came from him. Although William had his sympathisers amongst John's rivals, Dr. Joseph Priestly was satisfied that John had dealt fairly with William over Bersham. John eventually bought the Bersham ironworks and William's share of the proceeds was £10,650, a sum he could hardly have been expected to receive had the works been seriously damaged in a contretemps between the brothers. This was not, however, the end of the problems between the two brothers. Shortly after the sale of Bersham, Boulton and Watt decided to start up their own foundry for casting and boring steam engine cylinders. Hearing of the break-up of Bersham, the company asked William for plans of the specialised equipment there and he duly obliged by giving them drawings.

John had labour difficulties at Bersham about this time. Some of this might have been due to the uncertain situation caused by the squabbles of the brothers, but also iron founding was a rapidly developing industry with new firms starting up every year. Men experienced in making iron were in short supply and could easily be enticed to a new establishment by the lure of higher wages.

This being the case, it is difficult to know if men were leaving Wilkinson for higher pay or due to job insecurity. The Soho foundry of Boulton and Watt opened officially early in 1796 after a ceremony and an inaugural speech by Matthew Boulton. At such ceremonies it was usual for the founders to lay on food and drink for the workers. This particular ceremony must have been a jolly affair as there were over 200 participants who, it appeared, stole anything they could get their hands on – drinking cups, table cloths, cutlery, etc.

The partners themselves had difficulty getting skilled iron founders. Their foreman at Soho was Abraham Storey, who had worked for John Wilkinson at Bersham. Another of John Wilkinson's workmen, John Kendrick, began employment at Soho in April of that year. He asked for 21 shillings per week plus a house and fire with an additional two guineas for moving expenses from Bersham. All previous steam engine cylinders and cylinder bottoms from Bersham had been either cast by him, or under his care while working for Wilkinson, so he was quite a catch for Boulton and Watt. With the connivance of William Wilkinson, Boulton and Watt recruited several men from Bersham, then, in July 1796, showing great integrity, Watt wrote to Boulton stating that he thought this was unfair and that any more Bersham men who applied for jobs should be positively refused.

As other foundries opened up all over Britain the situation regarding the supply of skilled workers became critical. By 1797 John was laying off workers at Bersham. This was partly due to a lack of orders but was also because he was concentrating on the works at Brymbo, which was a better site. From this date operations at Bersham declined as the Brymbo site offered better transport facilities. By 1798 the Bersham works was mostly dismantled but continued with limited production until shortly after the deaths of both John and William in 1808.

The Brymbo estate, containing several farms, was purchased by John in 1793 and was farmed by him. This is not so strange as it seems. There was a great incentive for an ironmaster to obtain agricultural land and work it. At this time the horse was still the main means of moving goods. They were used as pack animals, for drawing wagons, hauling boats and barges, and for transport. Horses were also used in mines and for working machinery – the earlier gun boring machines were operated by horse gin.

Apart from pasture, horses need feed, as do people. In the 18th century and into the 19th century, the Corn Laws prohibited the import of corn until the home price reached a stated level. Corn prices would naturally rise following a bad harvest when supplies would be low; but the Corn Laws fixed the price so that it would be high even when there had been a good harvest. Food riots were common, as people attacked corn warehouses and mills to get at the grain.

Rioting was always accompanied by damage to property that was not necessarily associated with the storage or grinding of corn. One attempt to reduce the incidence of rioting amongst the populace was that introduced by magistrates in Berkshire in 1795 called the Speenhamland system. The central principle was that a working man had the right to a subsistence living and if, through circumstances not of his own making, he was unable to obtain enough through his labour, then society owed him the difference. Assistance, which was based on the price of a loaf of bread, would rise and fall according to market fluctuations. This was a popular system that was met with favour wherever it was introduced. There was a negative side, however, as the Speenhamland system tended to keep agricultural wages down. Although the Speenhamland system worked fairly well in agriculture, workers in industry soon abandoned it in favour of wage bargaining and the system was eventually superseded by the 1834 poor law.

As he could control the supply of corn by growing it on his own lands, John Wilkinson would have been better able to ensure supplies for his horses and for his work people, thus providing stability for his businesses. John was quite used to the management of land as, around 1777, he had bought the hill of Castlehead, near Grange-over-Sands, and the estate of Wilson House where his youth and early incursions into iron making had been spent with his father. Knowledgeable locals considered it to have been a foolish purchase as the surrounding land was peat bog that could not sustain saleable crops. Perhaps it was sentiment that took him there, but he set about building a country estate for himself and his wife then began improving the land for cultivation.

He built a house at Castlehead and commenced the planting of trees. As for the surrounding marsh, he had it drained by ploughing and spent huge sums adding clay, sand and mould to the surface, which he first had burned to remove the top layer. Because of the condition of the moss, the ploughs, at first, had to be worked by men as the hooves of horses would sink into the ground preventing them from hauling in harness. John soon got around this problem by making iron pattens of ten inches diameter that were fitted to the horses hooves to give them support on the soft ground. By the year 1805, a substantial tract of land around Castlehead, about 500 Lancashire acres, equivalent to roughly 1000 statute acres, had been claimed for agriculture and the land was successfully producing root vegetables including potatoes, barley, oats and rye. The rental value of the land had increased from less than one penny per acre when John first acquired it, to 30 or 40 shillings per acre per annum by 1805.

Hard work, the expenditure of time and money, but above all, John's indefatigable spirit, had produced success where everyone else had seen only failure. Without doubt, this part of the country had particular meaning to him, as it was here where he was buried in the grounds of the house he had built. Another reason for an ironmaster to acquire land was to facilitate transport. Where an industrialist wanted to construct a road or canal for the improved transportation of raw materials and manufactured goods, it would have to pass through land that was privately owned. If the landowner refused passage, or would not sell the required land, the plans would come to nothing. Often, a more circuitous route could be taken but this entailed greater cost. Right of passage over land (known as way leave) was a serious restriction on the development of efficient transport in the eighteenth century. The control of water supplies was a further important factor. Where water power was used, the construction of a weir was often necessary across a river or stream to maintain the water level. Holding dams and pools were necessary to conserve and regulate the flow of water to a water wheel. Landowners were jealous of their water rights and vigorously resisted any interference with the natural flow of rivers and streams. This might seem laudable to us today, but it is worth remembering that the eighteenth century landowner was not motivated to conserve the environment, but by a desire to secure his personal fishing and hunting rights.

As the new industrialists increased their wealth, the enormous amounts of money they could command made it easier for them to purchase land enabling them to do what they wanted without hindrance. Other difficulties existed for employers at the latter end of the eighteenth century, one of the most pressing being the supply of coinage for paying wages.

With the increase in manufacturing and the movement of labour from the land to the towns and other industrial sites, came a demand for more small denomination coinage. Agricultural workers were paid low wages with some of their income being given "in kind" in the form of accommodation and agrarian produce. Industrial workers had few, if any of these inducements, and required payment in coin. Where accommodation was specially built for industrial workers, they were charged rent, which had to be paid in cash.

In the last two decades of the eighteenth century the Royal Mint was having difficulty keeping up with the demand for copper coin. This was partly due to the mechanical limitations of stamping and partly due to fluctuations in the price of copper. The Royal Mint could produce enough coins in silver and gold without a problem, as industrial workers were hardly paid in these coins. The issue of gold and silver coin, and technically copper coin, was the strict prerogative of the Crown. Whereas some minting of silver and copper tokens was tolerated for a short period, the issue of gold coins was not permitted and there were severe punishments for unauthorised minting. Large manufacturers such as John Wilkinson, Boulton and Watt and others took to issuing their own "tokens". The system was not the same as for the later tokens issued by nineteenth century manufacturers to their workers, which could only be exchanged in designated shops usually owned by the mill owners themselves. Wilkinson's tokens, which were stuck for him in Boulton's mint at Soho, would be issued as wages along with official coinage and could be spent anywhere regionally. This was not the problem that it would be today. Workers rarely travelled far from their homes and places of work. All local shops and businesses would have taken the tokens as happily as they would official coinage so there was not the problem of profiteering and unfairness that would become associated with the "Truck Shops" of the nineteenth century.

Wilkinson is thought to have issued his own bank notes for a short time and even to have paid his workers in French notes. The success of Wilkinson's tokens is demonstrated by the number of forgeries that abounded at the time. Many of these can still be bought by coin collectors today. Most forgeries are easy to distinguish as the name is miss-spelt "Wilkison" or "Wilkeson." and some writers have thought that this was due to a colloquial use of his name. The copper token coins were mainly half pennies and had depictions of the various iron making processes on the reverse side, with John's profile on the obverse. A rare silver token had a ship on the reverse which is thought to have been issued to commemorate the launching of the Trial; although the actual rig was that of a brigantine, not a Severn trow. It could, though, have represented one of John's seagoing vessels. A copper token of 1787 shows a huge helve hammer in a forge and a workman holding a piece of metal over the anvil. A half penny token of 1790 shows a smith working metal at an anvil (perhaps he had Wayland in mind?). The token coin depicted here was struck in 1793. The obverse has the profile of John Wilkinson. Behind the anvil on the reverse can be made out the image of a sailing ship.

Wilkinson Coin (probably a forgery due to the improper spelling of his name)

IRON MAD

Shortly after his death, John Wilkinson became something of a legend among the folk working in the iron business. On a day in July, 1815, a large crowd gathered outside the gates of the Bradley Ironworks (some reports say as many as 2000). The story had got around that, exactly seven years after his death, John Wilkinson would return, mounted on his favourite grey horse, to see that his iron works were in good order. The event was recorded in a press notice of July 1815 and the survival of the tale testifies to the extent that John Wilkinson influenced his generation. Perhaps the people who lived and worked with him were infected by his "madness". As the disappointed crowd dispersed, many must have lamented with final acceptance the passing of "Iron Mad Wilkinson".

John Wilkinson died in 1808 at the age of 80. Although he had no surviving legitimate children, he did have three by his mistress, Ann Lewis, who was his housekeeper at Brymbo. The inscription below appears on the monumental obelisk at Lindale along with a cameo representation of his facial profile. It is believed that John composed this, his own epitaph, and it gives us some insight as to his character with the chief attributes being a commitment to hard work and faith in God. The epitaph is not complete as his executors deleted the first line. Interestingly, the first line read: "Delivered from persecution of malice and envy . . ." It seems that John had felt keenly the attacks made upon him by his rivals and perhaps by his brother too.

Here is his epitaph as seen on his obelisk.

JOHN WILKINSON
Ironmaster

Who died XIV July MDCCCVIII
Aged LXXX years

His different works in various parts of the kingdom
Are lasting testimonies of his unceasing labours.
His life was spent in action for the benefit of man;
And as he presumed humbly to hope to the Glory of God.

His life story is a testament to achievement brought about by labour, yet his attitude towards religion is much harder to reconcile with the sentiments on his epitaph. Known in his lifetime as "Iron Mad Wilkinson", his commitment to the universal use of iron in all areas became legendary. At several of his houses and work places he had an iron coffin that was for his own use should he die suddenly. These were sarcophagi intended to enclose a conventional wooden coffin. When John died he was buried four times! The actual story has improved in the telling and there seems to be some conflicting versions. However, all agree that his eventual internment was a protracted affair. He died at Bradley in Staffordshire and, while his body was being brought home to Castlehead, it had to be temporarily buried in the sands of the Morecambe Bay crossing due to the encroachments of the incoming tide. After it was dug out the next day, when his coffin reached Castlehead it was found to be too big to fit into the iron sarcophagus, so John had to be buried temporarily while a new one was cast. The third time he was successfully interred in the grounds of the house at Castlehead and a twenty ton, 40 foot high (12 metres) obelisk was erected over his grave. Even this, though, was insufficient to keep him in his grave. Some years later the house was sold. The new owner took a dislike to John's presence in his garden and had him disinterred and removed to Lindale churchyard where he rests today in an unmarked grave.

The obelisk lay for many years in a semi-derelict state, having been struck by lightning and left to rust into decay. Restoration began in 1983 when it was decided to erect it on the outskirts of Lindale on a mound beside the road to Grange-over-Sands. This scheme too, attracted controversy, as there were some in the village who objected to the obelisk and the cost to the parish in restoring it. It was as if the original first line of the epitaph had returned as a curse, but with grant aid, those campaigning for restoration won and it stands today, a proud memorial to one of British Industry's greatest and most colourful characters.

Those projects in which John pioneered the use of iron included an iron pulpit, door frames and window frames for a chapel in Bilston and, of course, the iron boat. He worked with Abraham Darby III on the Iron Bridge project. The parts for this were cast by Darby but John is known to have thrown his weight behind the scheme, which was undertaken in the face of stiff opposition. The world-famous Iron Bridge still stands today in the Shropshire town of that name.

An interesting invention of John's was the "iron man" that was to cut coal from a coalface. He intended that these machines should be used in his own mines at Bradley and Broseley but, so the story goes, his colliers refused to set the necessary roof supports saying: "if Wilkinson's iron men do the one they must do the other". Here is an example of the kind of dispute that was to run through industry to the present day - the introduction of machines to replace work formerly done by men. Apparently, John was able to steer clear of serious conflict with the government of the day, a circumstance that is difficult to understand given his political views and circle of associates. His renowned abilities as a businessman must have extended to politics, and although he is known to have had many enemies, none seem to have bettered him. That he had a very particular and forceful personality is evidenced by the apocryphal stories that grew up around his name after his death. Some of these tales are obviously embroidered, while others have a strong factual basis. That he felt the impact of malice and envy is indicated in the deleted line of his epitaph.

It was said that he never wrote a letter on any subject without the word "iron" appearing at least once. One story about him tells that once he had an idea he would think about it continually until he could discover the means of developing it. If the thinking process took several days then he would go without sleep until the problem was resolved. Once, a workman had to save him from falling into a vat of molten iron due to tiredness. Another tale has him lying in bed holding an iron ball (what else would it be) over a metal dish. If he fell asleep the ball would fall into the dish and awake him.

In 1958, a builder was demolishing a house in Highfields Road, Bradley, when he discovered that the structure was supported by a massive, wrought-iron beam. Panels in the front door were of iron as were the main staircase, roof beams, and tile supports. In addition, iron tie rods ran through the house wall-to-wall. Given the date of the house and the location, it is a fair assumption that it was built by Wilkinson to prove his faith in the universal use of iron.

Facts and tales about his love life seem to be at complete odds with his religious convictions. It is worth remembering, though, that manners and morals in John Wilkinson's day were very different from those of the Victorians whose morality was largely a reaction to the excesses of the eighteenth century.

Even so, the fathering of three illegitimate children, in the last eight years of his life, with his housekeeper at Brymbo, Ann Lewis, provoked a scandal which eventually caused the break-up of his fortune after his death.

The children were born to Anne while his wife (Mary) was still living at Castlehead. They were named: Mary Anne, Johnina and John and it was to Ann Lewis and these three children that he left his estate upon his death, his wife having died in 1806. John's youngest sister had married a man named Jones and their son, who changed his name to Wilkinson, contested the will on the grounds of illegitimacy, the children being born out of wedlock. The ensuing litigation persisted for years to the detriment of the business. Finally, after seven years of legal wrangling, the proceedings ended in the Court of Chancery when the Chancellor, Lord Eldon, reversed all previous decisions and found for the defendants. The children, however, hardly benefited as most of the value of the estate had been eaten up in legal costs. The nephew died some years later, a bankrupt.

With this sad business the story of John Wilkinson finally comes to an end. He had been one of the greatest ironmasters of his time, indeed Thomas Telford, who had discussed details of the Ellesmere Canal project with Wilkinson in 1793, called him "King of the Ironmasters." Clearly he was held in high regard by those of his contemporaries who were making the greatest contribution to the Industrial Revolution. His enemies seem to have been of lesser stature.

Today, Lindale is a quiet Lancashire village, which is passed through on the way to Grange-over-Sands, and there is little to cause the casual visitor to stop. Here, in the churchyard, John Wilkinson spends eternity, quiet at last inside his iron coffin in that part of England where his life's story had begun and where, as a boy, he had first poured the white-hot molten iron into his father's moulds.

BIBLIOGRAPHY

The Darby's of Coalbrookdale	Barrie Trinder
Wilkinson Studies Vol.s I-II	Various
Riots, Risings and Revolutions	Ian Gilmour
James Watt and the Steam Engine	Dickinson and Jenkins
England in the Age of Hogarth	Derek Jarrett
The Age of Oligarchy 1722 – 1783	Holmes and Szechi
The Lunar Society of Birmingham	Robert E Schofield
The Life of Joseph Priestly	Anne Holt
Ironworking	G K V Gale
The Medieval Machine	Jean Gimpel

Books By the Same Author

The Laurence the Armourer Series:

On Summer Seas – The Fighting Plantagenets
A Wilderness of Sea – The Rise of King Richard III
The Roaring Tide – A Tale of High Treason
The Doom Assigned – King Richard III In Victory

Other Books:

Who Wrote Marlowe – Christopher Marlowe Exposed

Web Site - www.quoadultra.net

Printed in Great Britain
by Amazon